Our Exciting Earth!

MOUNTAINS

By Jagger Youssef

Gareth Stevens PUBLISHING

Please visit our website, www.garethstevens.com. For a free color catalog of all our high-quality books, call toll free 1-800-542-2595 or fax 1-877-542-2596.

Library of Congress Cataloging-in-Publication Data

Names: Youssef, Jagger.
Title: Mountains / Jagger Youssef.
Description: New York : Gareth Stevens Publishing, 2018. | Series: Our exciting Earth! | Includes index.
Identifiers: ISBN 9781538209653 (pbk.) | ISBN 9781538209677 (library bound) | ISBN 9781538209660 (6 pack)
Subjects: LCSH: Mountains–Juvenile literature.Mountain ecology–Juvenile literature.
Classification: LCC GB512.Y68 2018 | DDC 551.43'2–dc23

Published in 2018 by
Gareth Stevens Publishing
111 East 14th Street, Suite 349
New York, NY 10003

Editor: Therese Shea
Designer: Bethany Perl

Photo credits: Cover, p. 1 Daniel Prudek/Shutterstock.com; pp. 5, 24 VarnaK/Shutterstock.com; p. 7 The World in HDR/Shutterstock.com; p. 9 Sharon Benton/Shutterstock.com; pp. 11, 24 B_Zuber/Shutterstock.com; p. 13 Vitalfoto/Shutterstock.com; p. 15 Ida Viktoria/Shutterstock.com; p. 17 YuriFineart/Shutterstock.com; p. 19 Taras Kushnir/Shutterstock.com; p. 21 luxora/Shutterstock.com; pp. 23, 24 gorillaimages/Shutterstock.com.

Printed in the United States of America

CPSIA compliance information: Batch #CW18GS: For further information contact Gareth Stevens, New York, New York at 1-800-542-2595.

Contents

Let's go to the mountains!

A mountain rises above the land.

A row of mountains is a range.

Some mountains have
a pointed top.
The top is called
a peak.

Animals live
on mountains.
I see goats!

Plants grow there.
I see pine trees!

People live there.
It can be cold!

Some people
climb mountains!

We drive
up a mountain.

We ski down!
Mountains are fun!

Words to Know

peak

range

ski

Index